FRANCIS
The Pope for Kids

John and Marieta Monette

Liguori

Imprimi Potest:
Stephen T. Rehrauer, CSsR, Provincial
Denver Province, the Redemptorists

Published by Liguori Publications
Liguori, Missouri 63057

To order, visit Liguori.org or call 800-325-9521.

ISBN 978-0-7648-2581-1

Liguori Publications, a nonprofit corporation, is an apostolate of the Redemptorists. To learn more about the Redemptorists, visit Redemptorists.com.

Printed in the United States of America
19 18 17 16 15 / 5 4 3 2 1
First Edition

FRANCIS

The Pope for Kids

By John Monette

Illustrations by Marieta and John Monette

To our beloved sons, Joseph and Joaquin,
and the baby on the way.

Born in a Country Far away

This is the story of Pope Francis.

It began a long time ago.

The year was 1936.
Just a few days before Christmas,
Jorge Mario Bergoglio
was born in Buenos Aires, Argentina.

Jorge Is Baptized on Christmas Day

Jorge received a very special gift that Christmas.

On the day we celebrate the

Son of God becoming a baby,

this baby boy became a child of God.

Jorge's Father, Mario

Jorge was the oldest son
of Mario and Regina Bergoglio.

His dad had moved from Italy to Argentina.

He worked as an accountant for the railroad.

Little Jorge loved trains!

and his Mother, Regina

Jorge's mother was a homemaker.

She raised Jorge, his two brothers,
and his two sisters.

She taught them to be good and to be kind to others.

She also taught them to love God and Mary.

Jorge Works as a Chemical Scientist

Jorge was very smart.

He went to school

and became a chemical scientist.

Here is Jorge busily at work

doing experiments in a lab.

God Calls Jorge to be a Priest

On the feast of Saint Matthew (September 21, 1953) Jorge stopped at a

church to go to confession.

Jorge said that during that confession,

"God came to me and invited me to follow him."

Jorge knew at age sixteen

that God wanted him to be a priest.

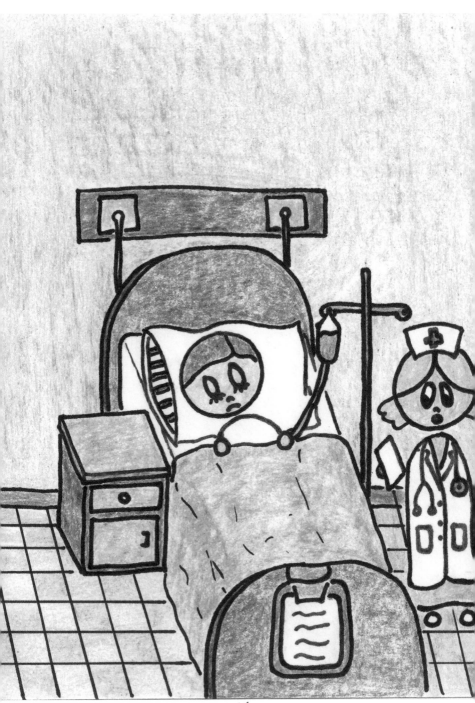

 # Jorge Gets Sick

When Jorge was twenty-one years old,
he got very sick.

He had to go to the hospital.

The doctors and nurses
took very good care of him.

Jorge says the nuns who worked
at the hospital helped him, too.
He got better again!

Jorge Joins the Jesuits

In March 1958, Jorge became a seminarian
in the Society of Jesus.
Seminarians study to be priests.

The Society of Jesus is a religious order
started by Saint Ignatius.

Life in the Seminary

As a seminarian, Jorge prayed and went to Mass.

There was time for playing sports and work.

Jorge studied a lot. He learned philosophy and theology. _Philosophy_ students

learn about nature and life. _Theology_ students learn about God and the

Church. Jorge taught others, too!

20

Jorge Becomes Fr. Jorge!

Four days before he turned thirty-three, on December 13, 1969,

Jorge was _ordained_. That means he became a priest. Now he could baptize

babies, celebrate Mass, and forgive sins in confession through Jesus! Now he

would be called "Padre Jorge" or "Father Jorge."

Jorge Is a Busy Priest

The next years of Jorge's life were very busy!

He continued training as a Jesuit and made his
final vows of poverty, chastity, and obedience.

After that he was a teacher, rector, and provincial.

A rector is the *priest in charge of a seminary
or a parish.*

A provincial is *in charge of a part of
his religious order.*

MISERANDO ATQUE ELIGENDO

Padre Jorge Becomes a Bishop

When Jorge was fifty-five years old, he became a bishop.

Here is a picture of his coat of arms.

The sun represents the Jesuits, the star represents Mary, and a plant called a _spikenard_ represents Joseph.

His Latin motto, "_miserando atque eligendo_," means "_by having mercy, by choosing him._"

Then He Becomes a Cardinal

In February 2001, Pope John Paul II made Jorge a cardinal!

Many people wanted to come to Rome and celebrate.

Jorge told them to give their

travel money to the poor to the poor instead.

26

Simple, Humble, and Poor

Instead of living in the fancy archbishop's residence,

Jorge chose to live in a small apartment.

He cooked his own simple meals

like chicken, vegetables, and fruit.

He Takes the Bus

Jorge could have traveled in expensive cars,

but he decided to use the city bus.

28

He Loves the Poor

Jorge loved the poor. He did all he could to help

them, like visiting them and bringing them things they needed.

29

Jorge Flies to Rome

When Benedict XVI said in February 2013
that he was going to resign from being pope,
Jorge flew to Rome to help elect the new pope.
But he was not planning to stay in Rome.

Jorge Votes for a New Pope

A _conclave_, a meeting of cardinals

who vote to elect a new pope,

began on March 12, 2013.

There were more than 100 cardinals

from all over the world!

No one got enough votes on the first day.

On the second day, the cardinals chose Jorge!

He was the new pope!

Jorge Chooses a Name

As pope, Jorge had to choose a new name.
His friend, Cláudio Cardinal Hummes, said,
"Don't forget the poor."
Jorge thought he would like a Church
that is poor and that is for the poor,
so he chose his name after
Saint Francis of Assisi,
who was called the "man of poverty."

Look, white smoke!
That means...

...Habemus Papam!
We Have a Pope!

Pope Francis walked onto the balcony overlooking Saint Peter's Square.

He asked the crowd to pray for him.

Then he gave his first blessing as pope.

a Lot of Love

Pope Francis shows us all a lot of love.

He puts other people first.

He does not want special things

like big cars or a big, fancy house.

He is close to those in need,

the sick, and especially kids!

 # World Youth Day

Pope Francis did a lot of things
in his first months as pope,
like leading World Youth Day.

World Youth Day is a gathering
of young Catholics from all over the world.
It was in Rio de Janeiro, Brazil.

People came together to pray,
learn about, and share their faith.

The theme was:
"Go make disciples of all peoples."

a Great Day at the Beach

On July 23, 2013, Pope Francis flew from Rome
to Brazil and got to meet the president of Brazil!

While he was in Brazil, the pope:
— celebrated Mass at the Basilica of the National Shrine to Our Lady of
Aparecida (a city in Brazil);
— cared for the poor in the Manguinhos slums;
— prayed the Stations of the Cross;
— and celebrated Mass with
three million young people on
Copacabana Beach.

The Light of the Faith

Pope Francis is a teacher.

He brings God's message to God's people.

He wrote two important letters:

The Light of the Faith and *The Joy of the Gospel.*

He wants us to share our faith with others

and learn more about Jesus.

Canonization of Two Great Popes

When the pope _canonizes_ someone,
that means *he is saying that person is now a saint.*

Pope Francis canonized two former popes:
John XXIII of Italy and John Paul II of Poland.

John XXIIII started the Second Vatican Council,
which encouraged a more modern way
of teaching our faith.

John Paul II worked for freedom for everyone
and encouraged people of all faiths
around the world to work together.

Dear Parents,

We hope that you and your children have enjoyed reading about Pope Francis. Here are some ideas for continuing their education in our faith:

1. Talk with your children about the pope and what our faith teaches about him. (He is St. Peter's successor and leads God's people).

2. Several virtues stand out in Pope Francis' life. Discuss them and why they are important. (He is humble and simple. He does not seek to have or enjoy possessions in this life. He believes our real treasures are in heaven.)

3. Pope Francis shows us how to love the poor and needy. Teach your children through your own example to look after others and to be generous with your time and money.

4. Pope Francis constantly asks us to pray for him. You can pray with your children for the pope and his intentions.

5. As a young man, Pope Francis listened to and followed Christ's call to become a priest. We parents should encourage our children to follow Christ wherever he calls them.

God bless you and your children,
Marieta and John
January, 2015